The U.S. Constitution

by Jean Kinney Williams

Content Adviser: Ken Clark,
Curator, The James Madison Museum,
Orange, Virginia

Reading Adviser: Dr. Linda D. Labbo,
Department of Reading Education, College of Education,
The University of Georgia

COMPASS POINT BOOKS

Minneapolis, Minnesota

Compass Point Books
3109 West 50th Street, #115
Minneapolis, MN 55410

Visit Compass Point Books on the Internet at *www.compasspointbooks.com*
or e-mail your request to *custserv@compasspointbooks.com*

Editors: E. Russell Primm, Emily J. Dolbear, Halley Gatenby, and Catherine Neitge
Photo Researcher: Svetlana Zhurkina
Photo Selector: Linda S. Koutris
Designer/Page Production: Bradfordesign, Inc./Biner Design
Cartographer: XNR Productions, Inc.

Library of Congress Cataloging-in-Publication Data
Williams, Jean Kinney.
    The U.S. Constitution / by Jean Kinney Williams.
        v. cm. — (We the people)
    Includes bibliographical references and index.
Contents: The goal: a "more perfect union"—Meeting in Philadelphia—Federalists and Anti-
Federalists—Two difficult issues—The presidency and the courts—Putting the Constitution into
place.
    ISBN 0-7565-0493-7 (alk. paper)
    1. United States. Constitution—Juvenile literature. 2. United States—Politics and govern-
ment—1783–1789—Juvenile literature. 3. Constitutional history—United States—Juvenile literature. [1. United States. Constitution. 2. United States—Politics and government—1783–1789.]
I. Title. II. Series: We the people (Compass Point Books)
    E303 .W455 2003
    342.73'029—dc21   2002155738

TABLE OF CONTENTS

NOTE: *In this book, words that are defined in the glossary are in* **bold** *the first time they appear in the text.*

THE GOAL: "A MORE PERFECT UNION"

"We, the People of the United States,
in Order to form a more perfect Union . . ."

These words are from the first line of the United States Constitution, the document that describes the country's government. In 1787, several dozen American men realized their unique opportunity to create a brand-new government after winning the fight for freedom from Great Britain. The result was

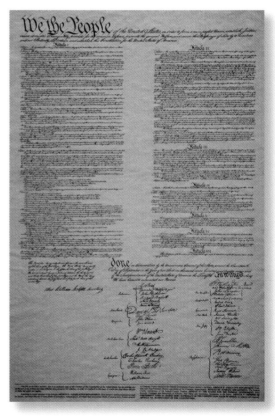

A reproduction of the Constitution of the United States. The original is on four separate pages.

4

the U.S. Constitution, a remarkable document that has continued to allow the United States to grow and develop. The Bill of Rights was added to the Constitution a few years later, in 1791.

Although the words *We, the People* express unity, behind them were weeks of arguing and compromise to create a government for the new, "more perfect" country. The Americans who wrote the Constitution won this battle, too. They formed a government that each of the thirteen new states would finally agree upon.

The original Bill of Rights

As colonies under Britain's rule, each state had developed into a distinct place. Each one had its own laws and customs. Northeastern states like Massachusetts and New York had busy seaports and bustling cities, and gradually they became antislavery. Southern states like Georgia and South Carolina depended on agriculture and black slave labor.

6

The original thirteen states

By the 1770s, all the colonies had agreed to break away from Britain. However, after the Revolutionary War (1775–1783) ended, getting the states to agree on something as important as new

New Yorkers in front of Federal Hall on Wall Street prepare for George Washington's inauguration there in 1789.

government and laws was a huge challenge.

The U.S. Constitution was the first constitution in history to limit the amount of power a government could have over its people. It is the world's oldest written constitution among major modern nations. While the United States may still not be the "perfect Union" its founders hoped for, under their Constitution the American people can keep striving for that goal.

7

A MEETING IN PHILADELPHIA

In the fall of 1786, a Massachusetts farmer named Daniel Shays was deep in debt. Shays led hundreds of other poor farmers in a rebellious march to Springfield, the state capital. The angry, desperate farmers demanded a tax break, and nervous Massachusetts politicians granted them one.

Daniel Shays led a farmers' rebellion in 1786 against government taxes.

Many government leaders throughout the new United States of America saw Shays' Rebellion as a wake-up call. There were no national laws to deal with rebellious mobs. What if an even larger uprising occurred?

Shays' Rebellion made government leaders realize the need for national laws.

Colonial politicians pray before a meeting of the Continental Congress in Philadelphia in 1774.

The Continental Congress, which first met in 1774, had steered the young country through the Revolutionary War. After the war, the United States operated with a loose set of laws called the Articles of Confederation. There was no national leader, however, and no laws existed to govern all the states.

Virginia and Maryland were squabbling over which state controlled parts of the Potomac River. Other states were operating like small countries—building their own navies, deciding whether or not (often not) to send money they owed to the Continental Congress, and making or breaking treaties with foreign countries or local Native Americans.

James Madison was a congressman from Virginia who had helped draft that state's constitution. When Virginia and Maryland argued over the Potomac River, Madison suggested that representatives from each state meet to solve the problem. After that successful meeting, Madison proposed that all the states have a larger meeting to work out other differences among them.

James Madison worked to resolve differences between the states.

11

Representatives from five states came together in the late summer of 1786 in Annapolis, Maryland. One of them was Alexander Hamilton, a brilliant young lawyer from New York who was concerned about the lack of a strong national government. Madison and Hamilton suggested yet another meeting. The Continental Congress invited delegates from all thirteen states to meet in Philadelphia the next year to discuss weaknesses in the Articles of Confederation.

Alexander Hamilton played a large role in forming a national government.

The meeting, known to history as the Constitutional Convention, was scheduled to begin in May 1787. It brought together fifty-five delegates from all the states except Rhode Island, whose representatives didn't want a stronger national government. Benjamin Franklin, by then an elderly man of eighty-one, was there to help represent

Benjamin Franklin represented Pennsylvania at the Constitutional Convention of 1787.

Benjamin Franklin (left) was one of six delegates to the Constitutional Convention who also signed the Declaration of Independence, which is being worked on here.

Pennsylvania. George Washington, who had led America's Continental army to victory over the British, had hoped to retire to his home at Mount Vernon, Virginia. However, he was asked to serve as leader of the convention, and he agreed. Thomas Jefferson and John Adams, both future U.S. presidents, were interested in the outcome of the convention but couldn't attend. They were away in Europe, representing America.

Many delegates to the convention had worked on state constitutions. More than forty of the delegates were members of the Continental Congress, and six of them had signed the Declaration of Independence.

It took some of the delegates weeks to get to Philadelphia. While waiting for the other delegates to arrive, Madison worked on what would be called the Virginia Plan. It was a guide for a new, national government to replace the existing confederation of states. He suggested a Congress, made up of two chambers. Members of these chambers would be elected by the people. Congressmen would then select members of two other branches of government—the judicial (judges) and the executive (the president and the president's staff). The federal government would decide what was legal or illegal for individual states to do.

Finally, by May 25, representatives from seven states had arrived. That was enough to begin the proceedings.

Philadelphia's Independence Hall in the 1870s

FEDERALISTS AND ANTI-FEDERALISTS

Everyone came to the convention prepared to make new laws, but not everyone wanted to create a powerful national government. George Washington favored a strong constitution because he believed thirteen feuding states would "soon bring ruin upon the whole." The delegates who supported a constitution and a strong federal government were called

George Washington supported the idea of a strong constitution.

Federalists and included Washington, James Madison, and Alexander Hamilton.

Those who disagreed with them were called anti-Federalists. One of the most outspoken anti-Federalists was Virginia's Patrick Henry. He had made history shortly before the Revolution when he declared, "Give me liberty, or give me death!" Henry protested the convention by not attending it. He and other anti-Federalists feared the loss of hard-won liberties under a strong national government. Would citizens end up at the mercy of wealthy politicians and their armies, who cared only about staying in power?

Patrick Henry was well known for his declaration "Give me liberty, or give me death!"

Federalists hoped to ease those fears with a reasonable plan for government. As former subjects of Great Britain, they were accustomed to the idea of basic individual rights and a government that represented its citizens, like Britain's five-hundred-year-old **Parliament.** European philosophers in the eighteenth century believed the government should both represent and serve its people. Another idea from that time called for separate and equal branches of government, so that no one person or group would have too much power.

Inspired by those ideas, colonists had thrown off British rule in 1776. Now Federalists had to convince their opponents that a strong American government would respect people's individual rights.

A meeting of the British Parliament in 1793

The purpose of the convention was to improve the existing government. As Madison's Virginia Plan was discussed, Virginia's governor Edmund Randolph suggested the possibility of creating a new government like the one proposed in the plan. Some delegates like South Carolina's Charles Pinckney wondered if that would mean the end of state government. Did this group have the authority to create a new government? On May 30, it was decided: The dele-gates would write a new constitution. Rather than patch up the Articles of Confederation, these men worked for the next three and a half months to com-promise their way to a new government.

Edmund Randolph presented Madison's Virginia Plan to the convention.

TWO DIFFICULT ISSUES

Two issues were especially hard to resolve—how to choose representatives to the new government and what to do about slavery. One of the first things the delegates agreed upon was to model the country's new government after the system already used by several states: There would be three branches of government. The *legislative,* or lawmaking, branch would be bicameral. That meant it would have two chambers of representatives from all of the states.

How would those representatives be chosen? Under the Articles of Confederation, each state had one vote in the Continental Congress. The Virginia Plan suggested using population to determine the number of representatives each state would have. Convention delegates from smaller states like Delaware worried that their state would have little power compared to a state like Virginia, which had ten times Delaware's population. Would Virginia or

The U.S. Senate in session during the 1880s

New York representatives be able to control the national government?

A committee of twelve delegates, one from each state, hammered out a compromise. The committee proposed that one legislative chamber be called the Senate and that each state, however large or small, would send two representatives. The other chamber would be called the

House of Representatives, and the number of delegates per state would be determined by each state's population.

Today, the two chambers together are called Congress. Their duties include making national laws, charging taxes, and deciding how to spend the tax money. State legislatures make their own state laws, too, but they can't pass legislation that disagrees with national laws.

Slavery was another difficult issue facing convention delegates. Many delegates from northern states wanted to

Southern states were dependent on slave labor.

23

abolish—or at least restrict—slavery, but they knew they would have to compromise to keep southern states in the Union. Tobacco, **indigo,** and rice plantations of the South had become dependent on slave labor. Delegates from states like Georgia and South Carolina would have left the convention if slavery was not allowed in the new Union.

Madison came up with a compromise on the issue of slavery. The population of a state would determine how many representatives it sent to Congress. Should states be able to count slaves, who had few or no liberties, as part of their population? Northern states said no, and southern states said yes. Madison suggested that southern states be allowed to count three-fifths of their slave population as part of their total population. The convention delegates also stated that Congress would not ban bringing new slaves from Africa until the year 1808. Northern delegates unhappily agreed that runaway slaves discovered in the North could be recaptured and sent back to their owners in the South.

After weeks of bitter debate, the issues of Congress and slavery were settled in what came to be called the Great Compromise. Looking back, we might wish that slavery had been more than just an "issue" to the delegates and that compromise had not been an acceptable solution. However, ensuring that all the states remained in the Union made it possible for future generations to guarantee "constitutional rights" for all Americans, regardless of their skin color.

Antislavery leader Wendell Phillips making a speech on Boston Common during the 1850s, many years after that issue was debated at the Constitutional Convention

THE PRESIDENCY AND THE COURTS

Convention delegates turned next to the executive branch of government and the court system. First, how much power should a chief executive have?

It was suggested that U.S. citizens should be the only ones to elect the president. Some delegates thought that the country was too large and widespread for all the voters to know the candidates well. So it was decided that each state would choose a group of "electors." The entire group of electors was called the electoral college, a system that still exists today. The number of electors per state is equal to the combined number of representatives and senators the state has in Congress.

States choose their own electors, who then cast their votes for president. Usually the general population and the electoral college choose the same president. Occasionally a candidate is elected president even after losing the people's

Delegates cheering at the 2000 Republican National Convention in Philadelphia, where George W. Bush and Dick Cheney were selected as running mates for that year's presidential election.

vote, otherwise known as the popular vote. This happened to George W. Bush in 2000.

Constitutional Convention delegates next discussed the kind of leader they wanted. South Carolina's Charles Pinckney thought the new country needed a "vigorous executive" to be a strong representative of America among

Benjamin Franklin suggested three presidents run the country.

other world leaders. Benjamin Franklin suggested three co-presidents who would each represent a different part of the country.

The delegates decided to have one leader, called the president, who would serve one four-year term at a time. The powers granted to the president included serving as commander in chief of the military, negotiating treaties with foreign nations, and granting pardons to people convicted of crimes.

The Constitution checks the president's power by requiring that two-thirds of the Senate approve the president's choices for **cabinet** members and judges.

28

On October 5, 1998, the House Judiciary Committee began hearings that led to the impeachment of President Bill Clinton. He was not convicted by the Senate, however, so he remained in office.

A president accused of misconduct can be removed from office by the **impeachment** process. The president can check the power of Congress by **vetoing** any law it passes. Congress can overturn the president's veto if at least two-thirds of its members vote to do so.

The delegates then turned to the third branch of the government they were creating: the judicial system, or the courts. They established a federal court system headed by

The Supreme Court heads the country's judicial system and meets in this building in Washington, D.C.

the Supreme Court, which is made up of judges who serve for life. The way judges would be chosen took longer to decide.

Some delegates argued that if Congress appointed judges, the selection process could become too "political." For instance, would members of Congress expect special favors for their states or for themselves in exchange for making someone a judge? On the other hand, allowing the

president to appoint judges would give him or her too much
power. The delegates settled on having the president appoint
federal and Supreme Court judges, but only with the Senate's
approval. Though it isn't in the Constitution, judges took on
the important job of deciding whether laws or decisions are
constitutional, or in agreement with the guidelines of the
Constitution. That power is called judicial review. The
courts also help settle disagreements among the states.

Members of the U.S. Supreme Court

ADMITTING NEW STATES

Another issue the Constitution's authors needed to address was admitting new states into the Union. Among the Continental Congress's last acts was the Northwest Ordinance of 1787. That legislation dealt with the land the United States acquired when it overthrew Great Britain. The Northwest Ordinance gave all newly admitted states the same rights as existing states.

The Constitutional Convention delegates wisely let that rule stand. Historians have since agreed that giving new states fewer rights than the first thirteen probably would have inspired more revolution.

President William Howard Taft signed papers in 1912 that admitted Arizona and New Mexico as states. Under the Constitution, new states have the same rights as existing states.

PUTTING THE CONSTITUTION IN PLACE

By now it was September. Delegates had spent the entire summer in Philadelphia. Without planning to, they had boldly created a new government unlike any that had existed before. This government was designed with its citizens in mind, not its rulers. The system of **checks and balances** in the three branches of government would prevent any one person or group from gaining total control of the country.

At the same time, the Constitution was broad enough to allow for future growth and change in government. For example, the Constitution granted Congress the power to pass any law considered "necessary and proper" for it to carry out its duties. More importantly, the Constitution was made the "supreme law" of the land—all three branches of the federal government, as well as state governments, must stay within its boundaries.

Not all of the delegates to the Constitutional Convention signed their names to the document they completed in 1787.

After so much compromise, none of the fifty-five delegates was completely happy with the document they had just finished writing. However, thirty-nine of them signed their names to it. As Benjamin Franklin said at the time, "Thus I consent, Sir, to this Constitution, because I expect no better, and because I am not sure it is not the best."

The Constitution would go into effect when it was ratified, or formally approved, by nine of the thirteen states. Each state had to organize a ratification convention. There, delegates chosen by that state's citizens would vote on whether to approve the Constitution.

As states prepared for that process, the debate for and against the Constitution raged throughout the land. It was argued in town meetings and in newspapers. Federalists had the important support of popular leaders such as George Washington and Benjamin Franklin. Alexander Hamilton, James Madison, and John Jay wrote several newspaper columns in favor of the Constitution. Their essays were later published in a book called *The Federalist*.

Anti-Federalists pointed out what they didn't like about the Constitution. One big

THE

FEDERALIST:

ADDRESSED TO THE

PEOPLE OF THE STATE OF NEW-YORK.

NUMBER I.

Introduction.

AFTER an unequivocal experience of the inefficacy of the subsisting federal government, you are called upon to deliberate on a new constitution for the United States of America. The subject speaks its own importance; comprehending in its consequences, nothing less than the existence of the UNION, the safety and welfare of the parts of which it is composed, the fate of an empire, in many respects, the most interesting in the world. It has been frequently remarked, that it seems to have been reserved to the people of this country, by their conduct and example, to decide the important question, whether societies of men are really capable or not, of establishing good government from reflection and choice, or whether they are forever destined to depend, for their political constitutions, on accident and force. If there be any truth in the remark, the crisis, at which we are arrived, may with propriety be regarded as the æra in which

A   *that*

A page from The Federalist

35

concern in Massachusetts was the lack of a bill of rights. In Virginia, Patrick Henry and others voiced fear of a government given too much power. However, anti-Federalists had no plan of their own to put forth in place of the Constitution.

Three states had ratified the Constitution by the end of 1787. Delaware was the first and was followed by Pennsylvania and New Jersey. Smaller states were more supportive of the proposed new government, while larger, wealthier states feared high taxes or the loss of liberties. In Massachusetts, ratification passed by fewer than 20 votes out of more than 350—and only after Federalists promised to work on adding a bill of rights to the Constitution. In June 1788, New Hampshire became the ninth state to ratify, putting the Constitution into effect as "supreme law."

Finally, in the summer of 1788, Virginia and New York ratified the Constitution. In Virginia, Madison also promised to support a bill of rights, but the vote in favor

A parade in New York City celebrating the passage of the Constitution in 1788

of the Constitution was still close. In New York, violence
broke out over the issue, and one person was killed.
Hamilton explained the Constitution to New Yorkers
from beginning to end, hoping to show its merits, and the
document was ratified by a margin of just three votes.

George Washington being sworn in as the first president of the United States

More than a year later, in November 1789, North Carolina approved the Constitution. It wasn't until 1790, a year after Washington became the first U.S. president, that stubborn Rhode Island became the thirteenth state to ratify the Constitution.

CONSTITUTIONAL AMENDMENTS

When the new Congress met for the first time in 1790, James Madison, author of much of the Constitution, introduced a list of rights to be added to it. Changes, or amendments, to the Constitution must be approved by the states, so Congress sent the twelve amendments to each state for ratification. Ten were adopted by the states, and they are the original Bill of Rights. The Bill of Rights is

The Bill of Rights permits protests such as this civil rights march in New York in 1965.

39

much more specific about the civil rights of U.S. citizens than the Constitution is. Those rights include freedom of religion, speech, and the press (news media). Other rights include the freedom to assemble peacefully and to petition the government.

Over the years, other amendments have been added to abolish slavery (1865), to give all men the right to vote (1870), and to give all women the right to vote (1920). A 1971 amendment gave eighteen-year-old citizens the right to vote. Altogether there have been twenty-seven amendments to the Constitution as Americans continue to build their "more perfect Union."

The Nineteenth Amendment gave women the right to vote in 1920.

William Gladstone, a British prime minister in the middle to late 1800s, called the U.S. Constitution "the most wonderful work ever struck off at one time by the brain and purpose of man." Americans growing up under the protective umbrella of constitutional rights should not forget the importance of that document. It was born of heated arguments and—ultimately—of the desire for justice and freedom.

The Declaration of Independence, the Constitution, and the Bill of Rights are on display at the National Archives in Washington, D.C.

GLOSSARY

cabinet—a president's group of advisers who are heads of government departments

checks and balances—ensuring that no one government official or branch has too much power

impeachment—the process of charging an elected official with a serious crime; it can result in removal from office

indigo—a plant that produces a deep-blue dye

Parliament—the part of the British government that makes laws

vetoing—refusing to approve, which prevents a measure from becoming law

DID YOU KNOW?

- Though he fought hard for ratification of the Constitution and served as secretary of the treasury, Alexander Hamilton couldn't run for U.S. president. According to the Constitution, only citizens born in the United States can serve as president. Hamilton was born in the West Indies.

- Thomas Jefferson (the third U.S. president) and James Madison (the fourth U.S. president) were such good friends that they wrote hundreds of letters to each other. Their letters were eventually collected in a book.

- Slavery was a controversial issue during the writing of the Constitution. Those who were against it were sorry and embarrassed they had to compromise. They didn't like making laws about slavery in a document describing U.S. citizens' rights and freedoms. So the word slavery never appears in the original articles of the U.S. Constitution.

- Slave owners George Washington and George Mason were among delegates to the convention who wanted to discontinue slavery. Washington freed his slaves in his will.

IMPORTANT DATES

Timeline

1765	Representatives from the colonies unite to discuss ways to deal with taxes they pay to Great Britain.
1774	The First Continental Congress meets.
1775	The Revolutionary War begins with the Battles of Lexington and Concord.
1776	The Second Continental Congress meets; representatives sign the Declaration of Independence on July 4.
1777	The Continental Congress drafts the Articles of Confederation.
1781	The Revolutionary War fighting ends; the Articles of Confederation are approved by all thirteen colonies.
1783	Great Britain and the United States sign the Treaty of Paris.
1786	Representatives of five American colonies meet in Maryland; Shays' Rebellion breaks out in Massachusetts.
1787	Delegates from twelve of the thirteen colonies attend a convention in Philadelphia; the delegates draw up a new set of laws—the U.S. Constitution.
1789	The Constitution takes effect as the law of the land.
1791	The Bill of Rights is added to the Constitution.

IMPORTANT PEOPLE

BENJAMIN FRANKLIN

(1706–1790), *talented and popular writer, scientist, and civic leader who was a delegate at the Constitutional Convention and a strong supporter of the U.S. Constitution*

ALEXANDER HAMILTON

(1755–1804), *brilliant lawyer who served as secretary of the treasury under President George Washington and was a firm believer in a strong national government under the Constitution*

PATRICK HENRY

(1736–1799), *Virginian and anti-Federalist best remembered for his cry of "Give me liberty, or give me death!" as the colonies prepared to free themselves from Great Britain*

JAMES MADISON

(1751–1836), *Virginian who was the fourth president of the United States and who is also known as the "Father of the Constitution"*

GEORGE WASHINGTON

(1732–1799), *Virginia planter who headed the Continental army during the Revolutionary War, was a leader at the Constitutional Convention, and the first president of the United States*

WANT TO KNOW MORE?

At the Library

Bjornlund, Lydia D. *The Constitution and the Founding of America*. San Diego: Lucent Books, 2000.

Feinberg, Barbara Silberdick. *The Dictionary of the U.S. Constitution*. Danbury, Conn.: Franklin Watts, 1999.

Sobel, Syl. *The U.S. Constitution and You*. Madison, Wis.: Turtleback Books, 2001.

On the Web

The United States Constitution Online

http://www.usconstitution.net

For the text of and background information for the Constitution, the Bill of Rights, and other U.S. documents

National Constitution Center

http://www.constitutioncenter.org

For information about the U.S. Constitution and the National Constitution Center in Washington, D.C.

Through the Mail

The National Archives and Records Administration

8601 Adelphi Road

College Park, MD 20740

866/272-6272

To obtain information about the U.S. Constitution, Bill of Rights, and Declaration of Independence

On the Road

Independence Hall

Independence Visitor Center

One North Independence Mall West

Sixth and Market Streets

Philadelphia, PA 19106

215/925-6101

To visit the place where the Constitution was debated and finally written

INDEX

About the Author

Jean Kinney Williams lives and writes in Cincinnati, Ohio. Her nonfiction books for children include several books in the Profiles of the Presidents series and books about American religions. She is also the author of *The Pony Express* and *African-Americans in the Colonies* in this series .